Restless Gold

Musings about California Pupils and Other Verses

David William Salvaggio

ARCHWAY
PUBLISHING

Archway Publishing books may be ordered through booksellers or by contacting:

Archway Publishing
1663 Liberty Drive
Bloomington, IN 47403
www.archwaypublishing.com
844-669-3957

ISBN: 978-1-6657-0484-7 (sc)
ISBN: 978-1-6657-0483-0 (hc)
ISBN: 978-1-6657-0485-4 (e)

Library of Congress Control Number: 2021906165

Print information available on the last page.

Archway Publishing rev. date: 04/08/2021

*"Everyone possesses
an element of profundity."*

–Lorraine Hansberry

This book is dedicated to the thousands of my former pupils who, over the course of thirty-five years, inspired me to write about them as well as myself.

Special acknowledgements to Mike and Jan Millspaugh. In the late 1990's, Mike, a Special Education teacher and Union Representative, pledged his support for me and joined me as an advisor to our first Gay-Straight Alliance. Both Mike and Jan encouraged me to keep writing and even assisted me in research for this book. Sadly, Mike passed in early 2019 and is sorely missed. And special thanks to all my former pupils who granted me permission to use their names or quotes and to Angela (wife of Dasan) who assisted me in research for this book.

CONTENTS

My Voice

Why does the world
Judge my voice so harshly?

Is it so intolerable,
    so loud,
    so foggy,
    so affected?

It is my only voice,
Impeded by a deaf ear
Parceled out at birth—
Mine until death.

Relax your phobias, unkind world;
My voice is now hushed.
My written words
Shall speak for me …

$\mathcal{P}\mathcal{K}$ Orange

A PK Orange is who I am,
"Preacher's kid," orange grove raised,
Always different—
Golden groves my sanctuary maze.

With laughter, I was called *queer*,
Battered, bruised, and taunted;
Kindred love so rare,
My childhood surely haunted.

Small and skinny,
Inept in water by a foul ear,
Sports Supreme chose me last—
My teens a painful path.

Religion gave me no comfort.
Father preached, "Queers to hell!"
I knew hell was already here;
To green groves, my sanctuary.

Yet from the groves emerged a winner,
Loving, happy, free.
Enlightened victor now; no sinner.
I'm me: I'm gay, I'm born again!

Golden Grove

Take her not from me,
The green and golden groves
I've always known,
For freeways, retail,
Or endless tract homes.

Low maze of bushy boughs,
She bears her ornaments quietly—
This, my childhood sanctuary.

Winter's smudge pots draw
Her white blooms
Beneath distant white peaks.

Spring yields her sweet bulbs
By braceros' gentle hands
As jackrabbits race by.

On foot, cycling, or driving,
I still choose her shaded roads.

Take her not from me,
The green and golden groves
I've always known.

First Day

My first day of teaching
In a full-time position:
Excited, grateful, nervous.

Will I get through to them?
Will my style they accept?
Will I appear inept?
Truly a rookie who appeared
Younger than my years.

Suddenly, a huge pupil
With massive arms, six foot eight,
Walked slowly toward me,
Looked down on me, a featherweight.

Will he strike me?
Throw me out the door?
He lifted me up horizontally
High up off the floor.

He lifted me up and down
Far above his head.
Now an actual barbell,
Fearful I might fall.

Suddenly, he put me down,
Now safe at my threshold.
Pupils smiled, giggled.
I knew then I could not scold.

The Zoo

In my crowded classroom—
Or as I call it,
The Zoo—
I often spot a select student
Staring at a map upon the wall.

His wide eyes following
Every boundary,
Every ocean,
Every landmark,
As if waiting for a call.

Gazing, thinking, daydreaming
Of where he'd rather be
Than in my crowded classroom—
Or as I call it,
The Zoo.

Silenced

"Stop it,
Or I'll call your mother,"
I often warned misbehaving pupils.

Sometimes, some pupils
Responded that Mom was single,
Lonely, and would like
A call from a man.

Silenced me like a Franciscan.

Scorned

Recently, Hester Prynne
Ambled into class,
Adorned with a
Twelve-inch scarlet *A*
Branded on her bosom.

"Why the *A*?"
I asked.

She wanted to feel
The pain Hester felt.
She wanted to know
The ridicule she knew.
She wanted to protest
What she protested.

The student wore
The *A* for
Two days
Wherever she went.

She even penned an essay
Of the taunts and laughs
Of others' stares,
Questions, and chaffs.

Her story
Spread so well
A news reporter

Published her tale,
Photographed the *A*
For all to tell.

Why this tale?
Many wondered.

"Literature changes lives"
Was my glad reply.

Black Hand

Thud!

His black hand,
Strong and agile,
Tossed *Huck Finn*
To the floor like litter.

Refused to read it;
His painful protest.

"I know—
I understand—
The N-word
Is wrong.

"Please pick it up.
Join us in our
Journey down Twain's river
Of realism,"
I pled.

He questioned
My reason.

"I promise,
By our journey's end,
You'll love Huck and Jim,"
I replied.

Slowly, reluctantly,
He reclaimed his text
And turned to chapter one.

Forty days later,
He aced the exam.

Goliath

Early in my career,
I often subbed for needed income
During my conference hour.

Assigned to an auto shop class,
I was surrounded by
Hard tools and tires amid
A stench of grease and gas.

Suddenly,
Goliath appeared at the door,
Angrily slapped a pipe
On his left hand.

The source and target of his anger
I could not know.

Tempted by fear to flee,
I forced myself to earn my fee.

Trembling within, I looked up.

"You are strong,"
I assured him.
"Very capable of harm.
Give me the pipe
To avoid more wrong."

To my surprise,
He relaxed his eyes of anger,
Slowly yielded
His weapon of lead.

He remained silent
As I called for help.

Fuckin

Today, I heard the word
Fuckin yet again—
And now, a teachable moment.

I took a deep breath,
Approached the board,
And wrote FUCKIN
In large caps with definitions:

    F = For
    U = Unlawful
    C = Carnal
    K = Knowledge
    I = In the
    N = Nude

I then lectured,
"A legend traces the word
From Old Irish law;

"Couples caught in adultery
Were punished with the word
FUCKIN on the stocks
Above them."

They understood all the words
Except *carnal.*

I directed a pupil to *Webster's*.
He wrote on the board:
Carnal = "physical; not spiritual."

Never heard *fuckin* again
In that class.

Faggot

Sometimes, the word *faggot*
Was yelled in my face
As I got on someone's case—

Another dagger in my soul
As my pupils sat in silence;

Another deep breath
As I moved toward the board
To fulfill another
Teachable moment.

I wrote the slur
In large caps
With my shaking left,
Then lectured,

"The word *faggot*
Comes from Old Europe,
Where bundles of sticks
Called *faggots*
Were used as kindling
To burn heretics."

My pupils sat aghast
As I penned the referral.

Never heard *faggot*
In that class again.

Tall TA[*]

Today, my big, tall TA
Threw his lanky left arm
Around my shoulders
When the bell rang
As we exited the room.

I looked up to my right;
His eyes briefly closed
With a smile so slight.
Then his arm withdrew.

Desirous of a dad?
Brother?
Friend?
Lover?

I'll never know;
But I know and feel
Such roles I cannot—
Must not—fulfill.

---

[*] Teacher's assistant

16 | DAVID WILLIAM SALVAGGIO

Falsely Accused

I cannot imagine
Anything worse than
A false accusation.

"Sexual harassment"
Was sometimes a retaliation
To my referral for
A dress code violation.

Next, the investigation
Brought an interrogation
Of fear, pain, indignation.
Finally, my exoneration.

Now, true empathy for
Those who stand accused.
Less quick to judge,
I retreat into solitude—

And a passion within me
To teach Hellman, Miller, and Lee.

Lovers

Today, I ate my lunch
Alone in my classroom.
Suddenly, something was amiss.
From my desk, I did zoom.

Out the window, I sensed my objection:
A clothed couple on a bleacher stand
Engaged in heavy affection,
Alone on their own island.

On my sandwich I nearly choked,
Shocked by the audacious pair;
The forbidden scene no joke,
Of two pupils in a lurid affair.

Their faces I did not recognize
As I pondered my possible action,
For behavior I could not authorize,
Nor sanction such public affection.

Open the window and shout?
As I reached for help on the phone,
Suddenly, the lovers vanished without.
My scrutiny quickly outshone.

Startled by a loud bell
For my fifth-period class,
I could now tell no one,
As I had no names to compass.

Suddenly, pupils poured into class.
"Hey, what's up?" they chimed en masse.

Freshman Boy

He claimed he had
Never read a book.

Never read a book—
Not in grade school,
Not in middle school.

No *Charlotte's Web*,
No Dr. Seuss,
No *Tom Sawyer*—

Only heard the teacher read.

After reading *Of Mice and Men*—
Heated discussion,
Thoughtful writing,
The dramatic film,
The boy nearly in tears—

He never knew a book
Could be so good.

Twins

Amid the rush of after-school traffic,
I spot a student walking home
Alone, with books in hand.
A warm tear wells within my eye,
Slightly blurring my view of him.

Today, he told me of his loss—
At age five, his twin fell victim
To a bank robber's fire.
Tall, strong, tenacious,
Their Spirit treads home.

The Artist

The pupil who defied me
Actually inspired me.

Often "forgot" his text—
But never his poster board,
Colored markers, pencils.

Instead of reading,
He listened
As his left hand
Created magic:

Loyal Huck and Jim,
Sexy Jay Gatsby,
Proud Hester Prynne
With her scarlet letter,
A spooky raven,
The House of Usher,
Guilty Lady Macbeth,
Nervous Blanche.

Though his name I can't recall,
His art adorned my classroom
For a decade, caught
The attention of all.

Rewarded

Two pupil authors won awards
In a local university's
Creative-writing contest
With 1,300 entries.

One timorous pupil
Penned poetry because
She felt it more confidently
Than speaking publicly.

She started her first-place poem
One day at lunch;
Rewrote it twenty times,
Described how we all
Switch masks throughout
Our lives.

The other pupil created short stories
For sheer enjoyment.
Her third-place fiction
Portrayed a young woman's conflicts
With her deceptive boyfriend.

She claimed writing
Rewarded her cathartically.

My reward: deep pride.

Desert Born

I'll never forget the day
In my hot valley classroom
After reading a poem about the sea,
A slight student in the back
Raised her humble hand—
She'd never seen the sea.

"Never seen the sea?" I replied.
"How can this be?"

Never smelled the ocean air,
Never heard the crashing waves,
Never splashed in the salty sea,
Never skipped upon the sand?

Desert born to a single mom
Who worked two jobs to feed
Her little girl who never saw the sea.

Years later, I still wonder if
She ever saw the sea …

Campus Couple

I can't help but gaze
Upon the campus couple,
Three years together,
Hands locked
Or arms entwined.

I recall the day they met
In my freshman class;
Now, seniors.

In class, they revere
Each other's words
As only truth.

He totes her books
As they pass
From class to class.

At lunch, they cling
To each other,
Eyes upon eyes.
Food and drink
They often ignore.

Saturday night fun
Finds them always
On the dance floor,
Destined to be one.

As I push thirty,
I can't help but ponder,
Why have I not found
A relationship so sound?

Skinhead

Within a sea of smiling faces,
A ferocious frown glares at me,
With large dark eyes
From a shaven head.

Clad in bags of cloth,
His huge frame struggles
For freedom from
A desk too small.

Suddenly, he breaks free.
This tank of armor
Rumbles toward me—
With hatred,
He flares loudly.

Gangbanger

"My Most Painful Moment"—
Today's essay assignment …

My tattooed Latino pupil,
Once trapped in his own
Cocoon,
Wrote effortlessly …

When a gangbanger,
He heard his mother
Weeping late one night
As he lay in bed.

He swore to himself
He would change.

The morning after,
The monarch emerged
Beautiful and free …

The Black Cat

"Anyone have a black cat?"
I asked my class.

Only one pupil affirmed,
With a question in her eye.

"My secret:
Just bring him tomorrow
In a carrier."

The next day,
All eyebrows raised
As I sat in my
Special teacher's chair,
Snuggled the large feline
With my right,
Balanced a book of Poe
With my left.

"Turn to page forty-four,
'The Black Cat,'"
I instructed the class.

Pupils and I took turns
In orally reading the dark tale.

Feedback:
Several adored the cat;
Many sickened by the plot.

Dazed

"Where's your belt?"
I asked a senior Adonis
As he sauntered into class.

His long, baggy pants
Sagged below his waist.

He claimed a girl
At lunch took it,
As his dark eyes
Cast a distant gleam.

He proudly proclaimed
Her love for him
With a wide grin.

"Hold up your pants.
Find your belt after class
If given the chance"
Was my command.

He agreed with a sigh
In a daze that was starry-eyed ...

Christopher

He was the only pupil
For whom I held open
The classroom door.

The purr of Christopher's motor
Disturbed us at first.
A victim of palsy;
A curiosity.

As time progressed,
So did we …

He liked Steinbeck,
As the author wrote about
The little guy, like him.

After a length of absence, I returned to find
No purr of his motor; pupils only wept.
In my roll book, I cringed to see
A sub* deleted his name and wrote, "Died."

---

* Substitute teacher

Condom and Cash

Yesterday, after class,
An unopened condom
Wrapped in a ten-dollar bill
Appeared on the floor
Under a pupil's desk.

Whose condom and cash?
I pondered.
The almighty seating chart
I consulted.

"A quiet boy of seventeen"
Was its rapid reply.

What action do I take?
Call a parent?
Write a referral?
What will be his fate?

After much thought,
The verdict was clear:
No laws nor rules broken,
No malice nor sin here.

Today, after class,
I called the pupil
To my desk,
Returned his condom and cash.

His head turned downward,
He smiled slightly.
Said not a word.
Left the room …

The Girl with Long Light Brown Hair

She sat in the back—
The girl with long light brown hair
And a kind smile.

A former pupil
Now on the TV news.
Her image and voice
Responded to my
Disbelieving eyes and ears.

"They weren't supposed
To shoot anyone;
The situation
Got out of hand."

She had joined
A teenage gang to plan
Armed robberies.

The victim—
Young Air Force nurse,
Mother of two.
Shot fatally in the neck.

My former pupil
Pled guilty—
Two counts of accessory to
Attempted kidnapping for robbery.

Served eight months
Of a one-year sentence.

The gang leader sentenced to death;
The shooter to life.

I can never erase the image and voice
Of the girl with long light brown hair
And a kind smile.

Tracy

Tracy adored cows
Like a child adores dolls.
Herefords, Jerseys, and
White ones dotted with
Big black spots.

Drew them,
Collected them
In photos, paintings, artifacts.

She was striking
Like Psyche of ancient folklore,
Long, flowing blonde hair,
An angelic smile evermore.

A fine pupil in my AP English class.
In our plays, a talented actress.

Then, late one night—
Crushed to death by an auto's
Drunk driver.

Following her wake,
All were invited to lounge
In her bedroom
Under the watchful eyes of
Herefords, Jerseys, and
White ones dotted with
Big black spots.

Highway One

Up the ragged coast,
My convertible purrs
Along the winding path
Called One, my Host.

From the rock to the ranch
By way of Old Harmony,
The wind calls to me
As living color flows by.

Rolling hills dotted with crooked oak.
Long, dark shadows cast
By spotted cattle amid
Wavering, golden poppies
Sparkling in the sun under the eye
Of a blue sky.

Pausing at Lucia's café and lodge
Where its perched views
Of a massive Pacific and sky
Become One.
Its rustic redwood cabins
With no television nor Wi-Fi.

Rambling northward
Beside an endless sea,
Reticent redwoods beckon
Before Steinbeck Country.

Along the boardwalk
To the Bay of Half Moon,
The city of chilled summers
In fog appears soon.

Blessed is my escape
Up the ragged coast
Along the winding path
Called One, my Host.

Sounds of Lucia

High upon an airy cliff
Perched upon the Golden Coast,
Along the winding Highway of One,
Sits the rustic lodge of Lucia.

Within its redwood walls,
I hear no television, nor telephone.
Without its redwood walls,
Listen, the simple sounds of Lucia.

Far below, a ceaseless roar
Crashes her white lace upon the rocks
As gulls' cries circle o'er.

Far above, her breath blows
A slow, cool mist easterly as
Peckers peck on crooked cypress.

Small colors flutter, hum busily
Upon buds of red and yellow as
Swift visions of blue mock closely.

All sanctioned by the Sierras
Of Santa Lucia herself
Just above …

High upon this coastal outpost,
Hanging on the edge of the world,
I hear no television, nor telephone.
Listen, the simple sounds of Lucia.

That Certain Summer

That certain summer, early in my career,
I had to work for needed income
In a haven of redwoods not so near;
Northward, under the giants so winsome.

As a teacher, I was hired
At a camp for privileged teens—
Children of the wealthy, most admired—
Above the Pacific, nestled in the greens.

The daughter of an actor
The son of a congressman
The son of a foreign ambassador
Even the daughter of a clergyman

Others were children of attorneys or doctors
Some the offspring of businessmen
Others the children of professors
Some considered by parents as a burden

At the weekly cost of a thousand-dollar payment,
Two or three weeks was the usual duration.
And while most were happy and innocent,
Some expressed serious abjection.

Six days a week, we staff labored
With one hour daily of freedom.
That one hour we always adored
Over the rules of our daily conundrum.

In our cabins, no food tolerated.
Only red swimwear at the pool or beach.
Scary ghost stories never narrated,
And complaints were an overreach.

While singing a song of the camp name,
Daily class schedules bustled.
Compliance was all part of the game.
While supervising activities, we hustled.

For nine weeks, I taught drama classes
For talented teens who could sing, act, dance.
Produced lively shows for the masses;
Pounded the ivories for each performance.

All staff were forced to participate
With a psychologist in weekly group sessions.
I surely resented this unfair mandate,
As we were pressured to answer personal questions.

Two girls in white dresses with not a pant nor short
Were summoned to the office of the dean,
Directed to procure attire for outdoor sport,
Jeans and shorts not to dry-clean.

No problem; not even a sigh.
They simply called Robinson's Department Store
And, with parents' credit cards verified,
Ordered for delivery Jordache and more.

One girl preferred no camp horse.
Called home to a parent,

Requested her own horse sent with no remorse.
Delivered the next day, to my astonishment.

One sad camper was with us all summer.
I asked if he was going home at week nine.
Not going home; a real bummer.
"Forced to boarding school" was his whine.

He never lived at home.
Placed in dorms and camps
By parents who traveled to Rome;
Left his mind and heart in cramps.

Since that certain summer of long past,
I've never worked again in a camp.
My summers crave freedom of overcast;
My life needs not another clamp.

September 11, 2001

The morning of
September 11, 2001,
Tense fear
Permeated the campus
As pupils pondered the perils
Of the sudden attack.

Fear swelled within me
As some non-Muslim pupils
Cast expressions of doubt, fear,
Even hate of my Muslim pupils.

The dark eyes of
My few Muslim pupils
Bore the pain of
Fear, rejection,
Isolation …

My daunting task
Now set before me—
I must teach the truth;
Most Middle Easterners
Are not terrorists!

Hot Sauce

Today, a pupil
Popped into class,
Placed a bottle of hot sauce
On his desk.

No textbook,
No pen, nor paper.
Only a bottle of hot sauce.

"Why the hot sauce?"
I asked.

Complained of
Cafeteria food—

Dry burritos,
Stale chips,
Hot dogs that taste
Like rubber,
Frozen pizza that tastes
Like cardboard.

No argument.

The Encounter

The most potent shock
Of my career
Transpired on a day
Just like any other …

Upon my daily routine
Of checking my mail
At my front-office box,
Something amiss appeared
Among the usual—
A page of college-ruled paper
Folded four times.

Such paper a daily sight,
But not its lurid contents.
For on it was written
An erotic message.

I gasped in disbelief
As I read the note
Printed in pencil—

A local phone number
Followed, anonymously.

Options flashed before me …
Do I turn this in?
Destroy it?
Remain silent?

I chose silence; no response,
And kept the note in my home.

Two weeks later, a second note
Appeared in my box—

I again chose no response,
But showed both notes
To my confidant and barber.

We both agreed the notes
Appeared sincerely penciled
By a male teen.

For decades, I kept both notes
In secrecy, until now.
They were discarded, with only
My barber as my witness.

Never heard from
That pupil again …

Adrienne

Born in Panama,
Her '88 grad photo
Reveals a stunning
Young lady with
Penetrating dark eyes.

Joined the Reserves
For the G.I. Bill
To become an attorney.

In Operation Desert Storm,
A scud missile hit her bunker
Late one night as she slept.
All members in her unit
Perished …

Never to be an attorney;
Never to be forgotten …

Stage Star

He encouraged me
To slap his face.

He played Tony
And I played Doc
In *West Side Story*.
The script required
I slap him.

Just couldn't do it.
One of my favorite pupils;
He held the voice, talent,
Physique of a Broadway star.

He even covered for me
One night when I forgot my lines.

I finally slapped his face,
Though I felt it more than him.

My Lesson Learned

Droopy eyes hung
Upon the pale face
Of a pupil as he
Staggered toward me.

As I reached for a pen
To issue a pass,
He threw his hands down
Upon my desk.

He tried to speak,
But only a sudden,
Forceful flow of green vomit
Spewed forth all over my desk,
Its roll book, grade sheets, records.

Its putrid stench
Permeated the classroom
As pupils gasped.

Months later,
Another pupil in another class
Staggered toward my desk.

I rose quickly, opened the window
Behind me.
Guided his head out the window,
Where a sudden, forceful flow
Of green vomit spewed forth
All over the pavement.

Our Angel

Early in my career,
I often wondered,
Will a pupil of mine
Become famous?

Tall, strong, handsome
Well mannered
Well spoken
Earned all As and Bs

On our baseball field,
An exceptional success
As a sly pitcher—
The pride of our school.

After graduation,
He emerged as an
Anaheim Angel—
Forever famous to all.

Wealth and retirement
Came early for this star,
But he never forgot us.

He returned often
For homecomings,
And to coach
Our young players.

While only one pupil
Became world famous,
Many of my pupils
Became "famous" to me.

Unwelcomed Caller

In the early '80s,
He was my class comedian.
Always smiling, laughing,
Upbeat, positive in
Class discussions.

Perfect for his part
In Ms. Barrett's class
In *Up the Down Staircase.*

Soon after graduation,
An unexpected, unwelcomed Caller
Came upon us …

A friend phoned me
Late one night;
Asked me to visit
The former pupil
In the hospital.

I could not, would not
Look upon the dark shadow
Cast upon the suffering face
Of one so young …

Decades later, I so regret
Not looking …
So wrong,
So very wrong …

And I'll never know
How and why I was spared the fate
Of the unexpected, unwelcomed Caller.

Choices

Lengthy essays,
Heated discussions
Of the topic
"Duties at home."

She was given no choice—
At age seventeen,
Forced by busy parents
To care for a newborn sibling.

She refused.

Secured employment by night,
Remained in school by day,
Rented her own apartment,
Maintained her high GPA.

Vanished

With a kind smile,
He counseled
Hundreds of pupils
Each semester;
Though rumors of him
Flew often.

If true,
Any negative side of him
I never knew.

Then, suddenly …
He vanished late one night
While camping in the
Brooding redwoods of Big Sur,
High above the ragged coast.

His wallet and keys left behind;
Never seen again …

Published Pupils

Today, a reporter
Came to my classroom
For photos and news …

Poems by ten pupils
Chosen from 70,000 others
For a national anthology
For only 1,500 entries.

Jennifer passionately pled,
"Help me out.
I'm being held hostage.
I'd mail myself away,
But I can't afford the postage …"

One pupil attempted to create
The sensation of victory
On a basketball court.

Another penned the perils
Of a friend's ordeal
In a custody battle.

Yet another composed
The emotions of love
For her boyfriend.

My pupils,
Now published writers;
My greatest gift.

Expressions

Another great gift to me
Was observing pupils'
Facial expressions
During those special moments
In literature.

When Romeo first saw Juliet
    George shot Lenny
    Annie worked Helen's miracle

When Caesar asked Brutus, "Et tu?"
    Huck fell in love with Mary Jane
    Naked boys killed Simon

When Macbeth's head rolled away
    Hester removed her *A*
    Huck told Jim, "Miss Watson died."

When Rose of Sharon fed a starving man
    George shot Gatsby
    Stanley raped Blanche

When girls chanted, "I saw Goody Goode!"
    Puritans hanged Rebecca Nurse
    Martha Dobie hanged herself

When Mayella testified
    Atticus counseled Scout
    Scout met Arthur Radley

Expressions of romance
    Shock and sorrow
    Victorious power
    Empathy and sympathy
    Disdain and disgust
    Relief and freedom
    Joyful justice

Literature is the best teacher of all.
She transports us in time,
Patiently describes settings,
Reveals characters,
Engulfs us in plots,
Engages us thematically,
Opens our minds,
Stimulates critical thinking,
Broadens our understanding,
Teaches us tolerance.

I am merely her lucky assistant.

Meetings

Long, boring meetings
Faculty meetings
Department meetings
Meetings with administrators
Meetings with parents

Verbose lectures
Repetitive reprimands
Heated arguments
Instructions for endless testing

And then committees
Textbook committees
Discipline committees
Committees to form committees

"Set me free" is my plea.
"Allow me to teach pupils
In my classroom
Without interruption,
Please …"

Tough Girl

Who is this tough girl
At only age fifteen?
Sits alone in the back
With a scowl upon her face.

Brings no book,
Seldom speaks,
Refuses to write
About herself.

She protests
It's too personal
As she glares at me.

Only age fifteen …

When Pupils Weep

The most powerful moment
In my career—
My unit on
Helen Keller.

Reading the script,
Lengthy discussion,
Writing …
Then, the movie
With Patty Duke
As Annie Sullivan.

"She knows! She knows!"
Annie rejoiced
As Helen's thoughts and words
Finally broke through.

Not a sound from my pupils.
Only tears flowed
From every eye …
Including mine.

Richard

Only eighteen, slender, and tall,
This roadrunner misjudged his path
As he raced his bike
To beat heavy traffic
As he crossed a busy pike.

Struck by a car,
He had no chance;
Passed instantly.

His wake was sad indeed,
Where many pupils grieved
And viewed their lost friend.

I approached the open coffin;
Viewed his handsome face
For the last time.

Recalled him in class—
Quiet, polite,
Excelled in math,
English lit not his might.

Why, oh God, I thought,
Is his young life gone?

I felt powerless, helpless;
Nothing but despair.
The sad fact that
Life is so unfair.

Yet, I am here,
Alive and allowed
To teach, grow old, and write.

The roadrunner became
An eagle in flight.

2000

How and why
Did the century's turn
Pass me by?

Hit like a landslide
With computers, passwords,
Cell phones, iPods,
CDs and iPads,
DVDs and tablets.

Then, iPhones,
Smartphones
With more passwords
To memorize and bemoan.

Now, it's …
"Turn off your phone!
Tablets on my desk!"
In my fair but firm tone.

Attendance and grades online,
Emails to receive and send,
Directives to download and print—
Is there no end?

More time for technology,
Less time for teaching …

Purple Hair

What happens to a pupil
Whose parents fled to Vegas
And never returned?

Placed in foster care,
She brings no book, pen, nor paper.
Wiggles with purple hair
And stares like an archer.

Rambles loudly
Before an altercation.
Complains abruptly
While in detention.

I must stop, listen, care.
And look beyond the purple hair.

Colorful Wads

"Get rid of your gum!"
Was my frequent rant.

Those annoying
Colorful wads
Stuck on desks,
Chairs, carpet,
My shoes …

"We have to
Chew gum for
Good breath to
Kiss our girlfriends,"
Philip explained.

"No kissing in here;
So get rid of it!"
I repeated.

Philip was intrigued
With reading Huck Finn.
His facial expressions,
Comments, essays
Bore empathy for
The abused truant,
Orphan, runaway.

A decade later,
Philip is a counselor

At his ole alma mater.*
Still empathetic for
Abused truants,
Orphans, runaways.

And still chewing gum …

---
* He's now assistant principal.

Home Invasion

Black, bold headlines
Glared back at my
Disbelieving eyes—

"Two Teens Arrested
In Double Homicide."
One, a student of mine
Of a few years past.

Accused of a
Home-invasion robbery
Of an elderly couple.

Both badly beaten;
The old man stabbed
In the neck.

I recalled
My former pupil—
A tall, big boy,
Quietly immature.

Both teens tried,
Convicted, sentenced
To life without parole.

My former pupil
Told his attorney,

"Please don't make
Any excuses for me."

He admitted responsibility.

His family wept like children,
As did I …

Mary

Mary was like a missionary.

A special-ed teacher
From another site,
She was called by me
To speak to our GSA*
And faculty.

At the century's turn,
She brought forth good news
Of Ed. Code 220—a new law
To prohibit discrimination
In California's public schools.

Strong, outspoken, fearless—
Welcomed by most,
Rejected by many.
Some staff walked out
In protest.

She represented me
When I filed complaints.

Falsely accused of lesbianism,
The loving wife and mother
Refused to cease her mission
Of truth and tolerance.

---

* Gay–Straight Alliance

Years later, she retired—
Invited me to be her friend.
Still never late
To preach against hate.

Envious of her children's blessing,
She's too young to be my mom,
Though I'll always regard her
As "Mother Mary."

Hungry

Her thin, cold fingers
Clutched the worn blanket
All around her
Shivering frame,
Clad in light attire
With only sandals;
No coat nor shoes
To her name.

She pled for food
After class.

My sandwiches
I gladly shared with her,
With a reminder
That breakfast and lunch
Were free.

That she could see,
But feared the taunts
Of others
For taking charity.

Transformed

Her stare of anger,
Sharp tongue
Pierced me
Like a dagger.

Consumed with ire
Until our unit on
A Streetcar Named Desire.

Toted her text,
Doted on each line.
Adored the movie,
Aced the exam.

First to sign up
For our field trip
To tearfully witness
The action on stage.

A quarter century later,
I still ponder an explanation
For her transformation …

Suicidal

Today, a counselor
Sent me an email—
A Latino member
Of our GSA*
Attempted suicide.

Crushed …
I can only ponder why
I failed to prevent
An act he tried.

So sad he tried,
So glad he survived.

---

* Gay–Straight Alliance

Homeless

She appeared normal—
Dressed well,
Sense of humor,
Popular.

I never guessed
She didn't have a home
Nor bedroom of her own;
Not even her own bed.

Her mom, siblings, and she
Migrated from their car,
House to house—
Friends, relatives …

Now a motel,
Not a Best Western
But one with
Carpets worn,
Toilet stained,
Curtains torn,
Door always locked.

Struggled to pay rent.
Mom urged her to
Quit school, get a job.
She refused.

Now working part-time
Nights, weekends.
Riding a bus.

Saving, searching, hoping
For a better place;
A better life.

Heroes

Getting pupils to read
Was often my dilemma,
Pondering the real need
Of my big, tall Olympians.

Some arrived with no text,
No paper, nor pen.
Only a blank look
With a ball in hand.

I then placed
L.A. Times sports pages
On my desk for them to see
News and photos of their heroes.

They grabbed the pages,
Read the news,
Gazed upon the faces of
LeBron, Kobe, Shaq …

Strategies

Endless strategies for teaching
Poor, middle-class, wealthy
Low-level, mid-level, and higher-level skills.

Immigrants
English learners
Physically challenged

Abused
Gifted and talented
Homeless

Gangbangers
Perfect angels
Delinquents

Three questions for educators—
Do you know your subject matter?
Are you excited about it?
Do you care about pupils?

If "Yes" to all three—
Success in education for thee,
No matter the strategy.

Barack O-Who?

The year was 2006.
Some black pupils complained
Of white-controlled government.

"Maybe not for long,"
I suggested to the teens as I held up
A popular magazine.

They pondered the dark face
Upon the cover.

"A young senator from Illinois,
Named Barack Obama,"
I announced.

"Barack O-Who?"
They amplified
While tongue-tied.

"Obama; he may be
Our next president,"
I surmised.

"No way!"
Some predicted
With panic in their dark eyes.
They feared a gun
Might be his demise …

Yes We Can

The morning after
November 4, 2008,
My black pupils
Sat quietly, but elated
With deep pride.

From Jim Crow to
Owens ...
Robinson ...
Parks ...
MLK ...
Jackson ...

They paved the path
To the House called White,
Built by ancestors of
The new president's wife.

With hope in their dark eyes,
Pupils asked if they could watch
The inauguration in January.

"Yes we can!"
Was my rapid reply
To their inquiry.

Foreign Exchange

He was my pupil from Germany.

Pressured by a campus skinhead
To attend a Nazi camp,
He refused with blue eyes
Of anger.

He asked me why
Some thought he was
A Nazi.

"They don't know history,"
I apologized.
"Vielen dank for your
Courage and patience."

He thanked me in German,
With a slight smile.

The Dreamer

Today, a Dreamer
Peddled tasty tamales,
Tediously crafted by the
Brown hands of his
Beloved Abuela.

He worried of others
Who sometimes
Laughed, teased him
For being here illegally;
Though he'd been here
Since he was three,
He confided in me.

"Don't give up,"
I pled.
"My classroom is your
Space free of strife …
I support your right
To a better life."

He thanked me in Spanish.

"Denada," I replied.
"Y manana?"

He promised tacos,
With a wide grin
Of his flawless whites.

Abused

Though I was struck thrice
By students on my back,
Head, and neck—

Far more annoying were
Some staff and students
With religious antics.

Religious books in the teachers' lounge
Preachy Bible verses in staff emails
Magazines, pamphlets in the restroom
Anti-Muslim flyers in my mailbox

Solicitations for Salvation Army volunteers
And to fund a teacher's summer mission.
A student letter to our school newspaper
Called us gays "sick, confused, in need of God."

A student once ditched her class
To preach to me during my free period.
Complaints were filed, with limited success.

A different kind of pain.

Faded Ones

Where did all my students go?
Callow pupils of long time past,
Juvenile figures, feeble and strong,
Winsome faces ever changing.

Amber, ebony, and in-betweens
Olive, bronze, and freckled white,
Children of the Earth these curious teens,
Hair auburn, sable, and towhead.

In dimmed bistros or a bustling fair,
On lengthy highways or in theaters,
Our paths might cross …
Students fade like sunsets,
Never to be seen … *

---

* Not long after I wrote this, former pupils began to appear—
especially via the new medium called Facebook.

First Email from the East

An email arrived today
From a pupil of a quarter century past
Who resides in the East.

She vividly recalled and thanked me
For "great class discussions"
Of literature.

Discussions of
Narcissus's rejection of Echo
Helene's tricks to marry Harry
Madeline's rape of Roderick
When Tessie won the lottery

Jane's devotion to Mr. Rochester
Depression over the lost Lenore
Buddy and his old cousin
When Granny confronted George

She now teaches literature
With "great discussions" in her class
And recalls my class of long past.

I replied with heartfelt thanks
For her kind words of memories past,
For her current work
In this valuable task.

Such emails,
As literature,
Always last …

Sharon

"I couldn't kill my baby,"
Sharon declared in a class discussion.
Boyfriend and she co-parented
To create a better situation.

She remained in school by day,
Worked full-time at night.
Still earned top grades
To graduate.

Quarter of a century later,
She spotted me at a class reunion.
Approached me, identified herself
For an evening of "memories" discussion.

Now Facebook friends.
And though we both believe
In the right to choose,
Sharon is a heroine
Whose choice is always good news.

Lorin

In a crowded Pasadena nightclub
Amid the loud, pulsing music,
From the darkness emerged
A muscular Adonis.

Could this be Lorin?
I pondered in disbelief.
My pupil of twenty years past!

My mind recalled him
In a flashback—
Slender
Smart with top grades
A fine actor
Highly regarded.

Now, Facebook friends.

Today, Lorin is married to Thomas
With two children so fine.
A corporate operations director
Outspoken progressive
An avid chef.

What an honor he remembered me.
Proud and pleased to know
He's in love, happy, and free.

Brent and Tonya

A special Facebook invite for me
Arrived today from Brent and Tonya:
"Come to Our '80s Reunion!"

From a quarter century past,
I well recall this cute couple.
Both striking blonds with high grades.

Both stole the show in *Up the Down Staircase*.
Brent the perfect Paul Barringer,
Tonya the best Bea Schachter,
Their talent bore the finest showcase.

Sometimes, class was a bore
For this young couple in love.
Their relationship on and off …

They married soon after graduation,
Later divorced and remarried.
Brent had a daughter and a son.
Some actions the basis of reflection.

They both divorced again later,
Realized their original error.
Married each other again.

They both love and adore
Their daughter and son.

Being together was their destiny.
Tonya an actress and magazine editor,
Brent in retail management—
Now, a level of serenity.

Anthony

"Welcome to UltraStar Cinema!
My name is Anthony,
And I have some reminders
Before the movie begins …"

Is that Anthony,
The kid in my class
Of two years past?
I pondered.

So quiet,
Shy, disinterested.
His assigned seat
In front of me.
Now a smiling speaker
In a public theater.

"Please silence your phones,
And enjoy the show!"
He concluded.

Why could I not
Motivate him to
Ask questions,
Give answers,
Earn higher grades?

Twenty years later,
Facebook friends,
Where I witness his
Life's journey …

Married to beautiful Rosalba
With two fine sons,
A lovely daughter.
Entertainment supervisor
For a major casino.

Though it was not me,
I rejoice that someone's
Efforts did succeed.

Sierra

Sierra must have inspected
A gourmet bistro or two
High up in the air
Where I dined in the
Sierras of Big Bear.

That was her profession—
A county health inspector.

A graduate where I taught
For three decades,
A natural beauty,
Lover of laughter,
Encouraging others,
And fun.

Then, suddenly …
Murdered
In a mass shooting
By two terrorists
Who lived two blocks
From my home.

Memories, photos
Of her smiling face,
Exotic flower
Atop her head,
Encourage us.

I still expect to see Sierra
Inspecting a gourmet bistro
Or two
Where her Spirit soars
Like an eagle
High up in the air
In the Sierras of Big Bear.

Angela and Dasan

A Facebook friend request
From Angela of
A quarter century past.
Her message to the point—
"I met my husband in your class!"

I well recall that special day.
Angela, a beautiful, blonde Caucasian,
Caught the roving, dark eye
Of Dasan, an Adonis African American.

I worried in fear:
What will their parents say
About this young couple in love?

Decades later, I am pleased to know
That Dasan and Angela married.
Their sweet union still aglow,
Their devotion still most primary.

Bore three talented sons,
All working hard in school.
Soaring as high as falcons
With unbiased love their wings.

Ra Ja

A Facebook friend request
Arrived today from a pupil
Of a decade past.

I well recall the Latino queen
In black attire,
Jet-black hair,
Porcelain skin with
Heavy black makeup;
Raised some students' ire.

Smart, kind, articulate
Though often absent
With low grades.

His counselor's urgent email
To his teachers:
"Be informed—
Rafael is a target of hate.
'Faggot' and such slurs
Do not tolerate."

When in class,
The rebel protested
For LGBT rights.
With his shout,
We both led that fight.
He's the reason
We cofounded

The first GSA*
In our city.

Now an adult, still in black,
Working hard,
In love,
Out of love.

Dancing in clubs by night,
Voting for Bernie,
Becoming a legendary diva
In her own right.

---
* Gay–Straight Alliance

Ashley

I could have sworn
Ashley was a lesbian,
Though she claimed
Bisexuality.

Strong, outspoken
GSA* president,
Campus crusader for equality.

Fifteen years later,
We're Facebook friends.

My computer screen
Shows me she's married
To a fine man
With whom she has twins
And a newborn.
Part-time waitress,
In college to be a teacher.

My eyes enlarged …
My mouth agape
In wonder …

---

* Gay–Straight Alliance

Pam and John

Former pupil Pam
Misses those note-passing days,
As she told me
Via Facebook today.

"Now, it's all texting
Back and forth,"
She mused.
"John used to pass me
Silly notes in your class."

I clearly recall
Those cute teens of
Thirty-nine years past—
Enrolled in my first
Full-time position's
U.S. history class.

Both bright blonds,
Pam scored As easily as I
Pushed John to excel.
Always smiling, laughing.

Dating began six years
After graduation.
Later, marriage.

Today, John and Pam—
Still married,

Still smiling, laughing,
As John is a computer whiz,
Engineer, "mad scientist."
Works for a major corporation.

Pam teaches elementary kids
While politically active;
Served as mayor pro tem
Of a major city.

Proud parents of three fine
Blond, blue-eyed sons;
Images of Pam and John.

Never suspected the note passing
Of decades past …
Such friendship grew
Into love to last …

Student Nurse

The young lady's announcement
Of my long, uncommon name
Echoed from the doctor's door
With perfect pronunciation.

She greeted me
After so many years;
Noted I still toted
My *Times* and Isherwood.

Learned to love reading
In my class …
Soon to be an LVN.
All this she mused
As she wrapped my left arm.

Too high

Encouraged me to
Think lovely thoughts
As she retried …

"Thank you for calming
Me today, my dear.
And your name?"
I asked.

She told me
With the same caring smile
I recalled from so
Long ago …

Only Sixteen

He was the handsome, quiet boy
Who sat in the back.

Only sixteen
When he grabbed a .22-caliber rifle
And, in repetition,
Shot his dad in the head.

According to his friend
Who helped dispose the bloody corpse
After the fact,
He held up a portion
Of the blown head and said,
"Look, brains."
And then cackled.

In court,
He pled not guilty,
Claimed physical, verbal abuse—
Acquitted,
Records expunged …

Three decades later,
Online searches reveal
He married, bore children,
Purchased a home …

Peter

"Thanks for all your help
In AP Eng. this year.
You're a very understanding teacher.
Take care and keep cool!"

Peter was one
Of only four pupils
Who signed my '93 yearbook.

Early signs
Of a true progressive—

For Ocean Waste Day,
He donned a dark plastic
Garbage bag
With another plastic bag
On his head,
Puka shells around his neck.

Vocalist, actor, dancer
Costarred with me
In *Bye Bye Birdie*.

Twenty-six years later,
Facebook tells me
He works and sings at
The University of Redlands
And is a youth director
In a progressive church.

I'm not surprised …

Obese Girl

As I lay curled
Up on my bed
With a warm cat
Snuggled next to me,
I see
The tall, obese girl
Of three decades past.

Sullen in her solitude,
Shunned by most,
Often absent—
An eventual dropout.

I spotted her one day
In the Ag. Dept.*
On the edge of campus,
Where few roamed.

With a slight smile
Upon her face,
She stroked the back
Of a fat cat.

I so desired to tell her,
And so I tell her now,
"I know,
I know ..."

---

* Agricultural department

Perfect TA[*]

The same every holiday—
A decorative box filled
With home-baked goods.

She daily asked for more chores,
Papers to check
Or scores to record.

"Done so soon?"
My usual response.

Matronly
Forever efficient
Punctual
Never absent

Though I've failed
To find her
Thirty years later,
I'll bet my perfect TA
Emerged the perfect
Wife and mother …

---

[*] Teacher's assistant

Daven

"You must have been
The student teacher
In my seventh-grade class!"
Wrote Daven
On Facebook today.

I grabbed a '78 yearbook
To confirm—
Forty years since
I gave his photo a look.

Vaguely recalled the quiet kid
Who sat in the back.

Now a world traveler,
New York Times best-selling author,
CEO, international speaker.

And he remembers me
A generation later?

Reyes

Reyes and I—
Now Facebook friends
Thirty-seven years later.

Active, friendly,
Outspoken …
The ham ad-libbed
In our production of
Up the Down Staircase.

"Your mama,"
He sassed Ms. Barrett
And brought down the house
With raucous laughter.

Came out as gay,
Now a radiology analyst
And proud daddy of three
Small, perky pups
And a curious cat
In stormy Seattle.

The Apology

Three decades
And five years
In the classroom,
Where many called
Me a "faggot"—

Verbally to my face;
Behind my back;
Written in textbooks,
On desks, doors, walls,
Or in notes.

Only one pupil,
A Latino teen,
Small in stature,
Apologized.

After a referral
And suspension,
He approached me
One day after class.

As he apologized,
He stumbled.
With big brown eyes,
He slightly trembled …
Offered his hand
To shake mine.

"Thank you," I said
To the pupil
Of years past,
"For your courage,
Which will last."

November 9, 2016

The morning after
November 8, 2016,
The worst of moods
Possessed me.

Now retired,
Only a prescheduled
Doctor's appointment
Forced me from
My home …

Suddenly,
My brown-skinned doctor
Entered the spotless room,
Considered the cause
Of my rising blood pressure.

"Last night's election,"
I lamented.

As an immigrant,
His dark eyes
Sympathized
As he pondered why.

"Complacency of many,"
I surmised.
"We must keep
Writing

Teaching
Preaching
Fighting
For justice and equality …"

The Redlands Bowl

A generation later,
Another unexpected, unwelcomed Caller
Has come upon us …

To the Bowl I retreat;
All shows canceled
As I sit alone
Amid rows of empty seats
To gaze upon a starry night.

Have you not noticed
A Special Show above?

A circle of towering hosts
Whose tops hug the stars
Guard carefully
An aged memory below.

Their bushy boughs shade few guests
By day
And rock gently to whispering winds
By night.

Check your hair and blanket;
Remnants may still be with you …

My Sanctuary

The Caller lingers ...
As no human shadows
Roam the walls of
Schools, libraries,
Cinemas, bistros ...

Not since '62
Have stores' empty shelves
Glared upon my eyes.

Told to stay home,
I grasp my
Times and Isherwood
Under my giant old fig tree,
Or
As I call it,
My sanctuary.

I lay languidly upon a lounge
And in the tranquil shade
Beneath a mass of green
With curious blue scrub jays,
And in the warm spring air,
I caress my faithful canine,
Grateful for my life
Under my giant old fig tree,
Or
As I call it,
My sanctuary.